CONTENTS

CONTENTS CREDITS

WAR BUDDIES

MONEY BACK GUARANTEE

SIX CHAPTERS LONG!

Lettering and Design by JOHN ROSHELL of COMICRAFT

Collected Edition Dustjacket A by **ALEX ROSS**　　Collected Edition Dustjacket B by **JIM LEE**　　Paintings by **TIM SALE & DAVE STEWART**

Special thanks to FRANK MASTROMAURO & NANCI QUESADA

The Folks From Helix Comics:
Aron Eli Coleite • Joe Pokaski • Jesse Alexander
Jeph Loeb • Chuck Kim • Mark Warshaw

NATURALLY NIFTY, NEWSY, NONDESCRIPT NONSENSE ABOUT OUR NUTTY NON-ENTITIES!

HEROES, published by WildStorm Productions. 888 Prospect St. #240, La Jolla, CA 92037. Compilation, cover art, chapter break art, interview and introduction copyright © 2007 Universal Studios Licensing LLLP. Heroes is a trademark and copyright of NBC Studios, Inc. All rights reserved. SUPERMAN #1 is ™ and © DC Comics. Used with permission. Originally published at www.nbc.com/Heroes/novels © 2006, 2007, NBC Studios, Inc.

WildStorm and logo are trademarks of DC Comics. The stories, characters, and incidents mentioned in this magazine are entirely fictional.

Printed on recyclable paper. WildStorm does not read or accept unsolicited submissions of ideas, stories or artwork. Printed in the United States.

DC Comics, a Warner Bros. Entertainment Company.

HARDCOVER

Alex Ross cover
ISBN-10: 1-4012-1705-2
ISBN-13: 978-1-4012-1705-1

Jim Lee cover
ISBN-10: 1-4012-1709-5
ISBN-13: 978-1-4012-1709-9

SOFTCOVER

ISBN-10: 1-4012-1707-9
ISBN-13: 978-1-4012-1707-5

MASSIVELY MIGHTY MASTHEAD:

JIM LEE
Editorial Director

JOHN NEE
VP—Business Development

HANK KANALZ
VP—General Manager:
WildStorm and
Collected Edition Editor

KRISTY QUINN and
MICHAEL McCALISTER
Collected Edition
Assistant Editors

ED ROEDER
Art Director

PAUL LEVITZ
President & Publisher

GEORG BREWER
VP—Design & DC Direct
Creative

RICHARD BRUNING
Senior VP—
Creative Director

PATRICK CALDON
Executive VP—
Finance & Operations

CHRIS CARAMALIS
VP—Finance

JOHN CUNNINGHAM
VP—Marketing

ALISON GILL
VP—Manufacturing

PAULA LOWITT
Senior VP—Business &
Legal Affairs

MARYELLEN McLAUGHLIN
VP—Advertising & Custom
Publishing

GREGORY NOVECK
Senior VP—Creative Affairs

SUE POHJA
VP—Book Trade Sales

CHERYL RUBIN
Senior VP—
Brand Management

JEFF TROJAN
VP—Business Development:
DC Direct

BOB WAYNE
VP—Sales

JUMP, MAGAZINE, SUNDAY.

THESE THREE WORDS describe a big part of my childhood and my imagination. They are three manga magazines published weekly in Japan. Even after coming to America at the age of six, I read the imported magazines and they defined a good part of my adolescence. These magazines printed stories by everyone from great classical authors like Osamu Tezuka and Fujio Akatsuka, to contemporary masters like Naoki Urasawa, Akira Toriyama, and Rumiko Takahashi, just to name a few. The artists always brought stories and characters that reflected our current culture and times to the page. We grew with them and they grew with us.

Manga, like graphic novels or any piece of art, has many unique powers. It can unite us and inspire us. Through these art forms, we share a common bond, a passion that we could all lose ourselves in. It was always fascinating to me that every Tuesday when the weekly SHONEN JUMP came out, all the businessmen, in their suits and ties, would pick up a JUMP from a kiosk. They would ride the subways or buses, all silent, just immersing themselves in

the world of manga. At that moment, these grown men were all experiencing the same thing. Manga is part of the Japanese culture and it defines a lot of who I am. At times it would be my romantic consultant, reading stories about a shy boy who is trying to muster the courage to ask a girl out. It would be my teacher as it pontificated on potential disruptions to the space/time continuum. It would be my hero as it continued to inspire me with journeys and tales of bravery and adventure. Sure, at lot of what I've "learned" isn't too applicable in real life, or would sometimes invite a slap in the face, but it enhanced my imagination and enriched our creativity.

We've all been affected by graphic novels in one form or another. As we grow, become adults, and gain responsibility, mangas are where I can find sanctuary and still be a kid. Imagination flows and it's a comfort to know that there are many, many others out there—from all walks of life—enjoying the same experience. If you're a kid, enjoy it. Savor it. Hold on to your imagination and your dreams. You can make a world

a different place—but it begins with you. If you're an adult, enjoy. Relax. Let yourself be a kid again. Take a vacation and let your mind wander in the magical world of graphic novels. No one can stop us from learning. No one can stop us from dreaming. No one can stop us from believing.

Tim Kring created a beautiful world, laden with rich stories and deep characters. Many artists came together under his vision to create a fantastical piece of television called HEROES. What you see on television is a reflection of all the hard work put in by hundreds of people. But a mere television show couldn't contain us. There still are more stories to tell, that we *wanted* to tell but couldn't given the medium. Fortunately, we can share and expand through a different medium. We present you these graphic novels to help add another dimension to the HEROES universe. We hope you enjoy it and let yourself get lost in the HEROES world.

For Charlie,
Hiro Nakamura
(Masi Oka)

SOMETHING IS HAPPENING.

MONSTERS

ARON ELI COLEITE ✦ MICHAEL TURNER & KOI TURNBULL

PETER STEIGERWALD & DAVID MORAN

MARK ROSLAN ✦ COMICRAFT

‹I TELEPORTED FIVE WEEKS INTO THE FUTURE. THERE WAS A BOMB... IT'S GOING TO DESTROY NEW YORK... MAYBE THE ENTIRE WORLD?›

‹I KNOW EXACTLY WHAT I MUST DO!›

‹WHERE DID I PUT IT?›

‹AHA!›

CHUCK KIM *Story*
MARCUS TO *Art*
MARK ROSLAN *Digital Inks*
DAVID MORAN *Colors*
COMICRAFT *Lettering*

IS LIFE EVER GOING TO BE *NORMAL* AGAIN?

I DIDN'T EVEN HAVE A GOOD *GUESS*. WHO WOULD *FRAME* ME LIKE THIS? *WHY?*

I GET IT. YOU'RE STRAPPED FOR *CASH*, TRYING TO KEEP YOUR *FAMILY* HAPPY.

HE DOESN'T KNOW THE *FIRST THING* ABOUT MY FAMILY.

COURSE, IF I HAD A WIFE THAT LOOKED LIKE *THAT*, I KNOW A FEW WAYS I COULD KEEP *HER* HAPPY.

AND HE *CERTAINLY* DOESN'T KNOW THE FIRST THING ABOUT *ME*.

DON'T *EVER* TALK ABOUT MY WIFE LIKE THAT *AGAIN*...

NIFTY *TRICK*, HOUDINI. LET'S SEE IF YOU CAN SLIP SO EASILY OUT OF THE *ROBBERY/MURDER* RAP.

WHAT'S *HAPPENING* TO ME?

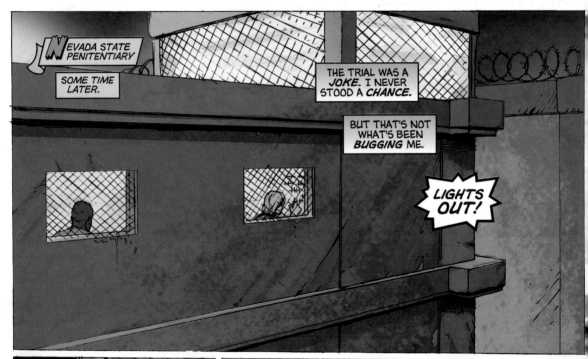

NEVADA STATE PENITENTIARY

SOME TIME LATER.

THE TRIAL WAS A *JOKE*. I NEVER STOOD A *CHANCE*.

BUT THAT'S NOT WHAT'S BEEN *BUGGING* ME.

LIGHTS OUT!

I KEEP THINKING ABOUT WHAT *HAPPENED* IN THAT INTERROGATION ROOM. DID I *IMAGINE* IT? WAS I POSSESSED? AM I GOING *CRAZY*?

HOW *DID* I GET OUT OF THOSE *CUFFS?*

MORE IMPORTANTLY, CAN I DO IT *AGAIN?*

C'MON DL. YOU CAN *DO* THIS. JUST REMEMBER, THIS IS FOR *THEM*. YOU NEED TO FOCUS.

ALL MY *ANGER*.

ALL OF MY *PAIN*.

ALL OF MY *LOVE...*

I REMEMBER TELLING MY *SON* ABOUT THE IMPORTANCE OF FOLLOWING *RULES*. GLAD HE CAN'T SEE ME *NOW*.

BUT I CAN'T *ROT AWAY* IN HERE, THINKING WHAT *COULD* HAVE BEEN. WATCHING MY OWN *BACK*.

SOMEONE NEEDS TO PROTECT *NIKI* AND *MICAH*. SOMEONE NEEDS TO FIND OUT WHO *FRAMED* ME.

SOMEONE NEEDS TO GET TO THE *BOTTOM* OF THIS.

IT'S NOT *FREEDOM*, I KNOW. IT'S JUST *ESCAPE*. BUT RIGHT NOW, IT'S MY ONLY SHOT AT GETTING MY *LIFE* BACK...

OKAY, SWEET-THING. *DL* WAS OUR SAFE-CRACKER. YOU PROMISED YOU CAN HANDLE THIS PART. YOU'D *BETTER* HAVE THE SKILLS.

OH, I HAVE THE *SKILLS...*

IT JUST TAKES A LITTLE FINESSE.

SOMETHING TO THE RIGHT.

THEN BLAH, BLAH TO THE LEFT.

AND... WHATEVER TO THE RIGHT.

OPEN SESAME.

KRR NN CH

FIVE HOURS AGO.

EVERYTHING WAS GOING SO *WELL,* AND THEN...

BUT I *STILL* NAILED YOUR WIFE.

CAN I REALLY *TRUST* WHAT I'M HEARING? WHAT DOES IT *MEAN?*

KRTAK

I WANT TO HEAR IT FROM *HER.* THE *TRUTH.* BECAUSE WHAT I HAVE NOW...IT'S SO *GRAY...*

THESE AREN'T FACTS...THEY'RE *THOUGHTS*...AND YOU CAN'T CONVICT ON A *THOUGHT.*

I NEED TO CLEAR MY *HEAD.* GO PATROL IN MY BLACK & WHITE. SORT OUT THE *RIGHT AND WRONG.* DON'T BOTHER WITH *MAYBES.*

ALL UNITS ON THE LOOKOUT FOR A *WHITE SPORTS CAR.* LICENSE #SOMA11 SUSPECTED IN *ARMED ROBBERY* OF LONGRIDGE SAVINGS & LOAN.

...NOW.

DUNTCH

NO DOUBTS.

DUNTCH

NO SECOND-GUESSING.

BOOM

JUST BLACK AND WHITE.

ISAAC'S FIRST TIME

ARON ELI COLEITE *Story*
MICAH GUNNELL *Art*
MARK ROSLAN *Digital inks*
DAVID MORAN *Colors*
COMICRAFT *Lettering*

Once upon a time...

...a Little Girl does her best to tune out an argument that's been going on for as long as she can remember.

In this household long filled with shouting, the Little Girl decided some time ago that it'd be best if she just kept quiet.

In fact, hardly a peep ever escaped her lips.

SLAM

LOOK WHAT YOU MADE HIM *DO.*

Her father didn't return that night, or any other.

"My Stepmother's right," she thought. "It is my fault."

"Not telling someone to stay is just like telling someone to leave."

She held on to the hope that her father might one day return --

-- though she was soon told that she did so in vain.

YOUR FATHER AIN'T *EVER* COMIN' BACK, SO YOU JUST PUT THAT *OUT* OF YOUR LITTLE OL' HEAD.

IF YOU'RE GONNA GO ON LIVIN' UNDER *THIS* ROOF, YOU'RE GONNA HAVE TO EARN YOUR *KEEP.*

And as immediately as her stepmother spoke, she was put to work.

EVERY DAY, RIGHT AFTER SCHOOL, YOU COME HOME AND GET RIGHT TO YOUR CHORES.

FIRST THING YOU DO IS VACUUM THE CARPETS.

Her life became an endless repetition of tasks carried out in silent servitude.

"Maybe if it's perfect," she thought. "Maybe then he'll come back..." And so she kept on.

As most adults know, life lived under the strict routine of work can pass you by in the blink of an eye --

All those years of suppressing her voice, keeping it deep down inside, made it so that when she finally spoke, no one could help but listen.

Her Stepmother's heart certainly listened, and stopped pumping the instant the command was uttered.

The Young Woman didn't know what power her voice held. She had changed in the course of an instant.

And nothing would be the same for her again.

Like her father had done those few years before, she left herself behind in that house now set ablaze.

"Move! You have to get out of here! Wake up!" she'd commanded.

But no matter what she said, she could not compel her Stepmother to move.

For what she ordered could not be undone.

And as she wiped away her tears, she wiped away her past.

ARE YOU *ALL RIGHT?* I'M GONNA CALL THE *POLICE.*

NO. JUST TAKE ME *AWAY* FROM HERE.

She had changed into someone else. Someone with a special gift.

WHERE DO YOU WANT TO *GO?*

WEST.

And to sever her new world of possibilities from the old, she decided to rename herself... Eden.

SALT LAKE CITY 125
LAS VEGAS 240

LIFE BEFORE EDEN

PIERLUIGI COTHRAN ✧ MARCUS TO
Story *Art*
MARK ROSLAN ✧ PETER STEIGERWALD *Colors*
Digital inks COMICRAFT *Lettering*

SHE'S *GOOD.* FEMALE INTUITION.

NO BACKUP. I'LL GO IT *ALONE.*

I'M GETTING *TIRED* OF THIS CAT AND MOUSE GAME.

YOUR HEART'S RACING, *FEAR'S* PUMPING THROUGH YOUR VEINS. DON'T DISAPPOINT ME *NOW,* AUDREY.

SYLAR!

I KNEW YOU'D SLIP UP *EVENTUALLY* AND I'D *GET* YOU.

OH, *NO!*

HE SET ME UP.

HE GAVE THIS POOR GUY HIS HAT AND COAT.

AND I *FELL* FOR IT.

I'M GONNA *GET* THAT BASTARD NEXT TIME.

SEE YOU IN THE *NEXT ONE,* AUDREY.

NO THANKS TO *YOU.*

WAIT, I'M *SORRY.* IT'S NOT MY *FAULT...*

DON'T ERASE EVERYTHING.

FATHERS and DAUGHTERS

ANDREW CHAMBLISS
Story

TRAVIS KOTZEBUE & MICAH GUNNELL *Art*

PETER STEIGERWALD
Digital inks

DAVID MORAN & JOHN STARR *Colors*

COMICRAFT *Lettering*

LEAVE THE *GUILT.*

NEW YORK CITY.

I'M SUPPOSED TO BE THE HERO. I SHOULDN'T BE HERE RIGHT NOW. LYING HERE IN A COMA. *DEFEATED.*

I DREAMT I WAS THE BOMB. BUT THAT'S NOT *ME.*

HERE. THIS. *THIS* IS ME.

THAT'S *The ROCKET.* HE USED HIS JETPACK SUIT TO ROB A BANK AND FRAME *ME* FOR IT.

YOU CAN'T **STOP** ME, PETER. AND YOU CAN'T CHANGE WHO YOU **ARE.**

NO. NOT **YOU.** NOT ME...

I'M SUPPOSED TO BE A **HERO.**

I'M **NOT** THE BAD GUY. I'M NOT THE **VILLAIN.**

I'M...

...THE HERO.

JERUSALEM, ISRAEL. 1967.

THAT'S MY MOTHER. *ZAHAVA.* YOU CAN'T TELL UNDERNEATH THAT FLIGHT HELMET, BUT SHE'S QUITE BEAUTIFUL.

SHE WAS ONE OF THE IDF'S FIRST FEMALE PILOTS.

SHE SHOT DOWN TWO *MIGS* DURING THE *SIX DAY WAR.*

I'M THE GAP TOOTHED GIRL IN THE MIDDLE. *HANA.*

A FAR CRY FROM MY MOTHER AND GRANDMOTHER'S LEGACY.

THE WARS WERE OVER. THE MAJOR BATTLES FINISHED. OR AT LEAST, THAT'S WHAT WE WANTED TO *BELIEVE.*

BUS

JERUSALEM, ISRAEL. 1989.

THE FIRST *SUICIDE ATTACK* IN ISRAEL OCCURRED WHEN ABD-AL-HADI GRABBED THE STEERING WHEEL OF A *BUS* GOING FROM TEL AVIV TO JERUSALEM AND FORCED IT OFF THE CLIFF AT KIRYAT YAARIM.

I WAS STILL IN THE HOSPITAL AS THEIR FUNERALS CAME AND WENT. I COULD NOT PAY PROPER TRIBUTE.

I COULD NOT SAY *GOODBYE.*

MY TANTA BRAVED *AUSCHWITZ.* MY MOTHER WAGED THE *WAR OF INDEPENDENCE...* THEY PLAYED BY THE RULES OF ENGAGEMENT AND *SURVIVED.*

THEN SOME COWARD CHANGED THE RULES FOREVER.

AND I HAD A *LEGACY* TO CARRY ON.

MOSSAD. ARMY INTELLIGENCE.

I ANALYZED. PLANNED *ATTACKS*. PLOTTED STRATEGIES. FOUND *WEAKNESSES*.

AT MY *BEST*, IT SEEMED AS IF I KNEW THE ENEMIES' MOVES BEFORE *THEY* DID.

THEY *PROMOTED* ME. AGAIN AND AGAIN. BUT I WAS STILL *MISERABLE*.

BUT I NEVER *GAVE UP*. I WAS DETERMINED TO SHOW THEM ALL EXACTLY WHAT I WAS *CAPABLE* OF.

EVERY NIGHT I WOULD WALK THE PERIMETER. IT WAS A WAY TO GET MY FIELD HOURS OUT OF THE WAY IN A NON-HOSTILE ZONE.

THE RULES OF ENGAGEMENT STATE TO *SHOOT ON SIGHT.* BUT THE RULES DIDN'T ACCOUNT FOR MY *HEART...*

...POUNDING IN MY EARS. AM I KILLING THIS MAN FOR SECURITY OR FOR *REVENGE?* AM I A PATRIOT OR A *MURDERER?*

I THOUGHT ABOUT MY MOTHER AND MY GRANDMOTHER AND...

...I HESITATED.

I *FAILED* THEM.

I'M NOT HERE TO *HURT* YOU, LIEUTENANT GITELMAN, I'M HERE TO *CHANGE YOUR LIFE!*

TEL AVIV, ISRAEL. 1992.

AFTER MY MOTHER AND GRANDMOTHER WERE KILLED, MY FATHER SENT ME TO A PSYCHOLOGIST.

FALL BACKWARDS. THEY'LL CATCH YOU.

YOU HAVE TO *TRUST* US, HANA.

THE PSYCHOLOGIST CLAIMED THAT I HAD *ABANDONMENT* ISSUES AFTER THE DEATH OF MY MOTHER AND GRANDMOTHER. HE SAID I NEEDED TO LEARN TO TRUST.

I NEVER HAD FRIENDS. *OR* BOYFRIENDS. I NEVER REALLY LIKED TO TALK. OR DATE. OR *WHATEVER*. AND THE TIMES WHEN I *DID* NEED SOMEONE...

...THEY ALWAYS LET ME DOWN. I DIDN'T *LIKE* THAT.

LOCATION UNKNOWN. TODAY.

AS I GOT OLDER I GOT *WORSE* AT HOLDING MY TONGUE.

YOU HAVE TO *TRUST* ME, HANA.

YOU CAN SEE HOW THAT MIGHT BE AN *ISSUE* WITH THE *BLINDFOLDING* AND ALL.

AND THE TESTS WEREN'T ONLY *PHYSICAL*. THEY MEASURED MY BRAIN WAVES. THEY POKED AND PRODDED. THEY TOOK SAMPLES AND INJECTED WHAT THEY CALLED "VITAMINS".

HE SAID I WAS SPECIAL, BUT I FELT *USELESS*. WEEKS OF TESTING AND STILL *NOTHING*. MY MOTHER. MY GRANDMOTHER -- I *FAILED* THEM.

YOU *PROMISED* I WOULD SEE ACTION, BUT ALL I'VE SEEN IS *SNOW!*

WE'RE DOING THIS TO *HELP* YOU.

HELP ME? I DON'T EVEN KNOW WHAT YOU'RE TESTING ME FOR? OR *WHY?* I WANT THE *TRUTH!*

WHO'S *THOMPSON?*

HOW DO YOU KNOW THAT NAME?

HE JUST SENT YOU A TEXT MESSAGE. I JUST *READ* IT. WHAT DOES THAT MEAN, *MANIFEST?*

HANA, MY PHONE HASN'T *RUNG*.

BZZZZZZ

From: THOMPSON

When will she mainfest?

I ALWAYS HELD BACK. I NEVER TRUSTED ANYONE, LEAST OF ALL *MYSELF*. AND THEN, IT WAS AS IF I OPENED A *DOOR*...

WIRELESS
Part Two

ARON ELI COLEITE & JOE POKASKI
Story

MICAH GUNNELL
Art

MARK ROSLAN
Digital inks

BETH SOTELO & PETER STEIGERWALD
Colors

COMICRAFT
Lettering

..AND A *FLOOD* RUSHED IN. ALL THE E-MAILS, TEXT-MESSAGES AND SATELLITE TRANSMISSIONS FLOAT *INVISIBLY* AROUND THE WORLD.

I DONT KNOW HOW IT WAS POSSIBLE, BUT I COULD SEE, READ, SENSE EVERY *ONE* OF THEM. EVERY *FYI* MEMO. EVERY SAPPY "I LOVE YOU" TEXT. CANS AND CANS OF E-MAIL *SPAM*.

I KNEW ANY CODE CAN BE BROKEN. YOU JUST HAVE TO IDENTIFY THE *KEY*. I KNEW WITH ENOUGH EXPOSURE, WITH ENOUGH PRACTICE I WOULD *MASTER* THIS.

IT WAS BEAUTIFUL... BUT IT WAS *TOO MUCH*.

ODESSA, TEXAS. TODAY.

I WAS NEVER MEANT TO BE *ORDINARY*.

HEY, DAD -- YOU'RE GOOD WITH *NUMBERS* AND STUFF...

I DID EVERYTHING I *COULD* TO MAKE MYSELF STAND OUT. TRAINED *HARDER*. STUDIED MORE.

LEMME FINISH THIS *CALL* AND THEN YOU AND I WILL ATTACK YOUR HOMEWORK.

BUT, AS HARD AS I *TRIED* -- AS MUCH AS I *WANTED* IT -- THERE WERE ALWAYS *OBSTACLES* IN MY PATH.

THANKS, DAD.

ALL THAT *CHANGED* THE DAY I MET THE MAN WITH THE *HORN-RIMMED GLASSES*.

HANA, ARE YOU *IN POSITION?*

97

TANZANIA, AFRICA.

HE SAID HE WAS WITH THE *C.I.A.* THAT I WOULD BE PART OF A *SPECIAL* GROUP OF OPERATIVES.

I'VE GOT TO GET CLOSE ENOUGH TO "*HEAR*" HIS COMPUTER.

DON'T GET *TOO* CLOSE OR THE MEN WITH *BIG GUNS* WILL COME OUT.

THE *HIM* IN QUESTION IS *DR. HENRY STRAUSS.* MICROBIOLOGIST. EVIL-SON-OF-A-BITCH.

DR. STRAUSS DISCOVERED A WAY TO ALTER *BACTERIAL-DNA* -- MAKING THE HARMLESS MICROBES IN OUR OWN STOMACH *DEADLY.*

OF COURSE, IF TREATED WITH ANTIBIOTICS, THE DOCTOR'S INVENTION IS *USELESS.* BUT MOST OF THE WORLD DOESN'T *HAVE* ANTIBIOTICS.

TODAY, DR. STRAUSS IS SELLING HIS FORMULA TO THE *HIGHEST BIDDER.*

THAT'S WHERE *I* COME IN.

WI-FI SATELLITE SIGNALS BEAM DATA ACROSS THE WORLD. SEEMINGLY *INVISIBLE.* BUT NOT TO *ME.*

I CAN SENSE THEM, READ THEM, STEAL THEM AND SEND THEM AND DESTROY THEM AS EASILY AS PUTTING PEN TO PAPER. MY CONTROL IS GETTING *BETTER* EVERY DAY.

THIS IS MY FIRST MISSION. MY FIRST OPPORTUNITY TO *PROVE* MYSELF. TO STOP THE BAD GUY. TO *SAVE THE WORLD.*

CH·CHNK

I GOT IT. NOW GET THE HELL *OUT* OF THERE.

BUT MY ABILITY STILL LEAVES MANY THINGS *OUT* OF MY CONTROL.

I WISH MY GRANDMOTHER WERE ALIVE TO SEE ME *NOW.*

I WOULD ASK HER, "HOW IN THE WORLD IS CONVICTION GOING TO GET ME OUT OF *THIS?*"

WIRELESS

Part Three

ARON ELI COLEITE & JOE POKASKI
Story

MICAH GUNNELL
Art

MARK ROSLAN
Digital inks

BETH SOTELO & PETER STEIGERWALD
Colors

COMICRAFT
Lettering

TWO MONTHS AGO.

WAS IT WHEN I FIRST NOTICED THOSE STRANGE *INCISIONS?*

ONE MONTH AGO.

WAS IT WHEN I FIRST LEARNED THAT I COULD SENSE *WIRELESS SIGNALS* -- LIKE SOME KIND OF *HUMAN COMPUTER?*

TWO MONTHS AGO.

OR WAS IT WHEN THE MAN WITH THE HORN-RIMMED GLASSES CAME OUT OF *NOWHERE?*

SIXTEEN YEARS AGO.

WAS IT MY DESIRE FOR *REVENGE?*

SEVENTEEN YEARS AGO.

OR THE DEATH OF MY MOTHER AND GRANDMOTHER?

TWENTY-ONE YEARS AGO.

WAS I TOO *INNOCENT?*

THIRTY-NINE YEARS AGO.

TOO *REVERENT?*

SIXTY-TWO YEARS AGO.

OR WAS I TOO *PROUD?* WAS IT JUST IN MY *BLOOD?*

104

NOW.

IT'S *EVERYTHING.* MY PAST. MY ABILITY. MY MISTAKES. I'VE BEEN FUMBLING TO FIND OUT WHO I AM. *THIS* IS ME...

...AND THESE *IDIOTS* SHOULD'VE SHUT OFF THEIR COMPUTERS.

AS I PUT MY PLAN INTO MOTION, MY HEART POUNDS. IT'S ME AND THE BUILDING AGAINST AN *ARMY.*

WHAT THE..?

I WAS IN IT *DEEP.* I WOULD BE ON AT LEAST TWO OR THREE GOVERNMENTS' *MOST-WANTED* LISTS. I WAS A WALKING *DEAD* WOMAN.

YET I NEVER FELT MORE *ALIVE.* FOR THE FIRST TIME, I KNOW WHO HANA GITELMAN TRULY *IS.*

MISSOULA, MONTANA. NOW.

HAVE A GREAT DAY, SAMANTHA.

THANKS, DOROTHY.

I CAN SEE THE EMAILS *CLEARER* UP HERE. MAYBE IT'S THE FRESH AIR, MAYBE IT'S A *MENTAL* THING, BUT...

...IF SOMEONE WERE COMING AFTER ME -- I'D *KNOW*.

I *LAID LOW*. NEW NAME. NEW *MISSION*. STAYED BELOW RADAR. NOT THAT I REALLY WORRIED ABOUT *THAT* MUCH ANYMORE.

I SPEND MY TIME TRYING TO FIND INFORMATION ABOUT THE MAN WHO *DID* THIS TO ME. THE MAN WITH THE *HORN-RIMMED GLASSES*.

HE USED ME. MANIPULATED ME. *CHANGED* ME. I'M GOING TO FIND HIM. MAKE HIM *PAY*.

AND I'VE JUST LEARNED THAT I AM NOT *ALONE* IN THIS SENTIMENT.

NOW, I KNOW WHAT YOU'RE THINKING. THAT I HAVEN'T *CHANGED*. THAT I STILL HAVE *VENGEANCE* IN MY HEART.

BUT, THAT'S JUST *WHO I AM*.

SALT LAKE CITY
LAS VEGAS
SANTA FE

THREE WEEKS AGO.

MY NAME IS *THEODORE SPRAGUE.* I CAN EMIT 10,000 Ci OF RADIATION FROM MY BODY.

WAY *I* HEAR IT, YOU'RE HIDING SOME SERIOUS *PLUTONIUM.*

THEY'LL PROBABLY GIVE US *MEDALS* FOR TAKING DOWN A *TERRORIST.*

I'M NOT A TERRORIST. I HAVE NO IDEA *WHAT* I AM.

TWO YEARS AGO.

I USED TO BE HAPPY. I USED TO THINK I HAD *IT ALL.* A SOLID JOB. THE PERFECT WIFE. A *HAPPY FUTURE* LAID OUT FOR US.

BUT, IT'S NEVER THAT *EASY* IS IT?

ONE YEAR AGO.

IT ALL WENT AWAY. THIS ABILITY KILLED MY WIFE.

I WAS A NORMAL GUY. I DIDN'T *DESERVE* THIS.

AND NOW I'M GOING TO BE LOCKED AWAY. I'M NEVER GOING TO LEARN WHO *DID* THIS.

THE ANGE IT *FEST* AND T

...IT EXPLODES.

HOW DO YOU STOP AN EXPLODING MAN?

Part One

JESSE ALEXANDER & ARON ELI COLEITE
Story

TRAVIS KOTZEBUE
Art

MARK ROSLAN
Digital inks

BETH SOTELO
Colors

COMICRAFT
Lettering

HANA TOLD ME HER *STORY*. GROWING UP IN ISRAEL. *MOSSAD*.

THE SAME PEOPLE THAT GOT TO *ME*, GOT TO *HER*. THEY GAVE HER *ABILITIES* TOO. USED HER. *ABUSED* HER.

SHE AND I WANTED THE SAME THING. *REVENGE*.

THIS IS THE *NEEDLE* THEY USED ON US. YOU USED TO WORK IN *PHARMACEUTICALS*. YOU CAN *TRACK THIS DOWN*. BECAUSE --

WHAT? WHAT ARE YOU *SEEING?*

YOU'RE IN *DANGER*. YOU'VE GOT TO GO. *NOW!*

SOMEWHERE IN THE NEW MEXICO DESERT.

MY NAME IS *THEODORE SPRAGUE. TED.* I CAN EMIT 10,000 Ci OF RADIATION FROM MY BODY.

I'D BEEN *HUNTING* FOR THE MEN WHO GAVE ME THE ABILITY TO UNLEASH *ATOMIC HELL.* TEN SECONDS AGO, THEY FOUND *ME.*

WHAT THE HELL DO YOU *WANT?*

I'M HERE TO PUT YOU OUT OF YOUR *MISERY,* TED.

WHY IS HE SO *CONFIDENT?* DOESN'T HE KNOW I COULD WIPE HIM OFF THE FACE OF THE EARTH?

HOSE HIM!

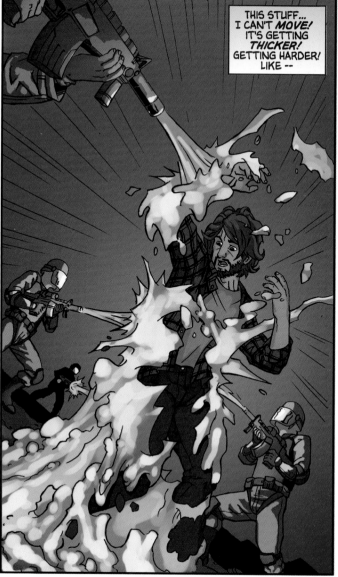

THIS STUFF... I CAN'T *MOVE!* IT'S GETTING *THICKER!* GETTING HARDER! LIKE --

115

116

-- PAYBACK!

AFTER THE EXPLOSION, I SEARCHED FOR THE MAN IN CHARGE. HE *MUST* HAVE SURVIVED.

BUT THERE WAS NO *SIGN* OF HIM. *ANYWHERE.*

HE MUST'VE *FLED*, LEAVING HIS DEAD MEN BEHIND.

NO MATTER, I STILL HAD THAT CLUE FROM *HANA*, THE MYSTERIOUS WOMAN WHO COULD HEAR THE *INTERNET* IN HER *HEAD.* SHE CALLED HERSELF *WIRELESS.*

HOW DO YOU STOP AN EXPLODING MAN?

Part Two

JESSE ALEXANDER & ARON ELI COLEITE
Story

JORDAN KOTZEBUE
Art

MARK ROSLAN
Digital inks

BETH SOTELO
Colors

COMICRAFT
Lettering

TWO DAYS LATER. BILLINGS, MONTANA.

JUST LIKE *ME*, WIRELESS BORE THE NEEDLE'S UNIQUE MARKS ON HER *NECK*.

Pharmatech Industrial Building

SHE GAVE ME THE SCHEMATIC OF A HYPODERMIC GUN, WITH *TWIN NEEDLES*. I LEARNED IT WAS MADE INSIDE THIS *BUILDING*.

I WAITED 'TIL THE *WEEKEND*, FEWER *PEOPLE* WOULD BE AROUND. FEWER PEOPLE IN CASE THINGS GOT...

I WONDER WHO *HE* IS? DOES HE HAVE A WIFE? A *FAMILY*? SHOULD I LEAVE? OR IS HE *PART* OF THIS?

WHILE MY *BRAIN* WANTS ANSWERS, MY *HEART* SEEKS --

-- REVENGE!

I ASKED HIM WHAT THE HYPO GUN WAS *FOR*. DID THEY USE IT TO *CHANGE* ME? TO MAKE ME INTO A *FREAK*? I WASN'T READY FOR HIS ANSWER.

THE HYPO GUN IS USED BY WILDLIFE RESEARCHERS. THEY *TRANQUILIZE* THEIR PREY, THEN USE THE HYPO GUN TO INJECT THE BEAST WITH A SPECIAL *ISOTOPE*.

THIS ISOTOPE CAN BE *REMOTELY DETECTED*. ALLOWING THE RESEARCHERS TO *TRACK* THE ANIMAL WHEREVER IT GOES.

WAS THAT WHAT I HAD *BECOME*? A *WILD ANIMAL* TO BE TRACKED AND STUDIED? GUESS I COULD *RUN* --

-- BUT I COULD NO LONGER *HIDE*.

119

To Be CONTINUED...

AS VEGAS, NEVADA.

CLASS, TODAY WE'RE GOING TO LEARN HOW TO *SHARE FILES*.

COMPUTER CLASS IS MY FAVORITE TIME OF DAY.

I RELATE TO THEM. MAYBE IT'S BECAUSE I CAN TALK TO MACHINES.

OKAY, EVERYONE CLICK OPEN THE *FOLDER* ICON ON YOUR DESKTOP.

BUT I KEEP THAT A SECRET. YOU NEVER KNOW HOW SOME PEOPLE REACT TO SOME SECRETS.

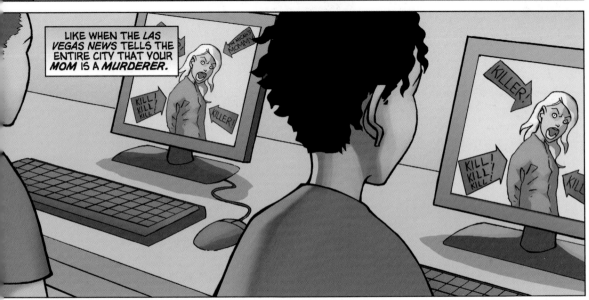

LIKE WHEN THE *LAS VEGAS NEWS* TELLS THE ENTIRE CITY THAT YOUR *MOM* IS A *MURDERER*.

THE TEACHER PROMISED TO FIND WHOEVER WAS RESPONSIBLE...

BUT I DIDN'T BELIEVE HER.

SO I WENT STRAIGHT TO THE *SOURCE* AND ASKED IT.

I KNOW YOU *DID* IT, FRANK. YOU PUT IN THAT FILE. AND I'VE GOT *PROOF.* SO JUST *STOP* IT. OKAY. BECAUSE IF YOU *DON'T,* I'M GOING TO SEND IT TO THE *PRINCIPAL.*

BULLY

CHUCK KIM
Story

MICAH GUNNELL
Art

MARK ROSLAN
Digital inks

BETH SOTELO & PETER STEIGERWALD
Colors

COMICRAFT *Lettering*

POW

FIGHT! FIGHT! FIGHT!

WE DON'T *WANT* YOU HERE.

YOU BELONG IN *JAIL* WITH YOUR PSYCHO KILLER *MOM.*

WHAM

IN HINDSIGHT, MAYBE NOT THE *BRIGHTEST* MOVE.

BUT IT FELT *REALLY GOOD.*

HE'LL *NEVER* FIND HIS WAY OUT OF THERE. LET'S *GO.*

NO WAY! THAT LITTLE TURD'S GONNA TAKE A *POUNDING.*

124

AAAAAAAHHHHH

IT'S LIKE I *SAID*...

YOU NEVER *KNOW* HOW SOME PEOPLE ARE GOING TO REACT TO SOME SECRETS.

*S*ANDERS RESIDENCE.

YOU GET IN A *FIGHT* AT SCHOOL TODAY?

IT WAS *NOTHING*. JUST SOME *JERKS*, THAT'S ALL.

JUST WANT TO KNOW IF YOU *WON*, THAT'S ALL.

YEAH. I *WON*.

TWO DAYS AGO.

ODESSA BUTTON WORKS

ODESSA GAS

CAPTURED, TORTURED, THEN INJURED. IN *PODUNK,* TEXAS.

THESE BULLET HOLES WOULDN'T BE A *PROBLEM* IF I HAD JUST GOTTEN THAT *CHEERLEADER.*

HER DADDY WAS A DAMN GOOD *SHOT* FOR A GUY WHO NEEDS *CORRECTIVE LENSES.*

BUT NOT GOOD *ENOUGH.*

I CAN'T IMAGINE HE'S *NOT* COMING AFTER ME. AFTER WHAT I DID TO HIS *DAUGHTER.*

NOT TO MENTION HIS *WIFE.*

I NEED TO GET AS *FAR* AWAY FROM HERE AS POSSIBLE.

WHICH MEANS I NEED A *RIDE.*

BEER

I HAD *NO IDEA* HOW TO DRIVE A TRUCK.

BUT, AS CHANCE WOULD *HAVE* IT, I RECENTLY ADDED ANOTHER *ARROW* TO MY QUIVER.

WELCOME TO THE *BURNT TOAST DINER.*

CHANDRA SURESH RECENTLY IDENTIFIED A *WAITRESS* IN MIDLAND, TEXAS WHO LIKELY HAD A *SPECIAL ABILITY.*

BERRY GOOD *MEMORY!*

I DON'T KNOW, I JUST SEEM TO BE *REMEMBERING* THINGS LATELY.

I WATCHED HER *ALL MORNING,* UNTIL IT BECAME CLEAR WHAT THAT ABILITY *WAS.*

SOON AFTER I *KILLED* HER, I DON'T KNOW...

I JUST SEEM TO BE *REMEMBERING* THINGS LATELY.

VVVMMMMMMMMMM

BEER

YOU BLOW OFF A *ROUTE* AND I SUPPOSE PEOPLE START MISSING THEIR *BEER.*

THIS IS THE *LAST* THING I NEEDED.

THERE'S NO WAY I'M *PULLING OVER.*

THE STATE OF VIRGINIA SEEMS TO THINK *OTHERWISE.*

THEY HAVE *NO IDEA* WHO THEY ARE *DEALING* WITH.

TIME TO LET THEM KNOW I'M NOT YOUR *ORDINARY TRUCKER.*

I SUPPOSE THEY'RE BEGINNING TO *UNDERSTAND* THAT.

THERE'S ONLY *ONE WAY* OUT OF THIS. AND I NEED TO TIME IT *PERFECTLY.*

VVVMMMMMRRRRRRR

ROAD KILL

JOE POKASKI
Story

JASON BADOWER
Art

ANNETTE KWOK *Colors*
COMICRAFT *Lettering*

NOBODY'S GOING TO EXPECT A *SURVIVOR.*

AND IF THEY *NEED* A BODY, MY FRIEND IN THE *TRAILER* WILL DO.

I *HATE* GRAVEYARDS. THEY'RE MUSEUMS FOR AWFUL MEMORIES.

SOMETIMES IT'S BEST *NOT* TO THINK. THOUGHTS CAN ONLY *WEIGH DOWN* THE SOUL.

MATT PARKMAN AND TED SPRAGUE ARE GOING TO HUNT DOWN THE MAN WITH THE *HORN-RIMMED GLASSES* -- THE MAN WHO CHANGED *ALL* OF OUR *LIVES*.

IF THEY *THOUGHT* ABOUT IT, THEY WOULDN'T GO. IT'S *FOOLISH*. REVENGE AND EMOTION MAKE EXCELLENT *BLINDFOLDS*.

ME, I'M ON A *DIFFERENT* PATH.

THE MAN IN THE HORN-RIMMED GLASSES IS GETTING HIS ORDERS FROM *SOMEWHERE*.

WITH MY ABILITY, I CAN SEE *WIRELESS COMUNICATIONS*. E-MAILS. TEXT MESSAGES. *THAT* SORTA THING.

I SAW A *STREAM* OF ENCRYPTED E-MAILS COMING OUT OF *ODESSA*.

I'M DONE THINKING. I'M JUST *DRIVING*. FOLLOWING THE STREAM. AS IF IT WERE THE FRIGGIN' *YELLOW BRICK ROAD*.

AND WHEN I PULL BACK THE *CURTAIN*... I'M GOING TO FIND THE WIZARD THAT'S BEEN *MANIPULATING* US.

The PATH of the RIGHTEOUS

ARON ELI COLEITE *Story* **STAZ JOHNSON** *Art* **CHRIS SOTOMAYOR** *Colors* **COMICRAFT** *Lettering*

IT'S HARD TO FILTER IT OUT. THE SEA OF *DATA*. LOVE LETTERS. BUSINESS TRANSACTIONS. EMOTIONLESS AND BRUTAL. THIS POOR GUY JUST GOT *DUMPED*. THAT *SAD GIRL* IS SO LONELY.

I TRY TO *IGNORE* IT. TRY TO STAY ON MY PATH. *FOCUSSED.*

BUT, FOR ALL MY *BIG TALK.* FOR ALL MY CONVICTION. I MADE A *MISTAKE.*

I *THOUGHT.*

HE'S GOING TO *HURT* HER. *SOMEONE* HAD TO SAVE HER. I'M THE ONLY ONE WHO SAW WHAT WAS GOING TO *HAPPEN.* HOW CAN I STAND IDLE?

THIS ISN'T WHAT I *WANTED* TO DO. THIS IS WHAT I *HAD* TO DO.

137

TEXAS. AFTER MIDNIGHT. 1992.

IT WASN'T THE *FIRST* BAG AND TAG THAT I'D RUN WITH CLAUDE.

THIS WOMAN WE'RE AFTER, HAS SHE MANIFESTED AN *ABILITY?*

NOT A *CLUE.* BUT THAT'S THE *FUN,* RIGHT? NEVER KNOWIN' *WHAT* WE'RE GONNA GET.

WE'D BEEN PARTNERS FOR A WHILE. I WAS STILL A ROOKIE. HE WAS THE *PRO.*

ISN'T THIS *DANGEROUS?* NOT KNOWING WHAT WE'RE WALKING *INTO?*

"WE'RE" NOT WALKING INTO ANYTHING. *YOU'RE* STAYING OUT HERE AND KEEPING *WATCH* LIKE A GOOD DOGGY, WHILE *I* DO THE HEAVY LIFTIN'.

CLAUDE COULD MAKE HIMSELF *INVISIBLE.* I THINK THAT MADE HIM FEEL *UNTOUCHABLE.*

BUT WHAT IF SHE *SPOTS* YOU?

IT'S FORTY WINKS PAST *2 AM,* ROOKIE. AND I'M BLOODY *TRANSPARENT.* SHE'S NOT GONNA SPOT ME UNLESS I SAY *"BOO."*

ON MOST JOBS, CLAUDE WOULD *SNEAK IN* ON HIS OWN, AND *TRANQUILIZE* THE TARGET, WHILE I WAITED OUTSIDE...

...FOR THE *"ALL CLEAR."*

KABOOM

AND AS THE DOOR PELTED ME IN THE *CHEST*, AND THE HEAT FROM THE *FLAMES* SINGED MY SKIN, I *WONDERED*...

...IF AN *INVISIBLE MAN* CATCHES ON FIRE, CAN YOU SEE HIM *BURNING?*

HELL'S ANGEL

JESSE ALEXANDER *Story*   MICHAEL GAYDOS *Art*   EDGAR @ STUDIO F *Colors*   COMICRAFT *Lettering*

THAT WAS THE FIRST TIME I *SAW* HER. A LITTLE ANGEL IN HELL. MY *CLAIRE*.

AT THAT MOMENT, I COULDN'T KNOW THAT CLAIRE WOULD SOON BECOME MY *DAUGHTER.*

BUT I KNEW *ONE* THING FOR CERTAIN.

I WOULD DO *EVERYTHING* IN MY POWER TO KEEP THIS CHILD *SAFE.* NO MATTER THE *COST.* NO MATTER THE *CONSEQUENCE.*

ANY IDEA HOW TO CHANGE A *DIAPER?*

NONE. BUT I COULD USE A CHANGE OF *UNDERPANTS* MYSELF.

DON'T WORRY, CLAIRE. *I'LL* PROTECT YOU.

ODESSA, TEXAS.

MY ADOPTED DAUGHTER JUST WALKED UP TO A *NUCLEAR MAN*, AS HE WAS ABOUT TO GO HIROSHIMA -- AND KNOCKED HIM *UNCONSCIOUS*. SHE SAVED THE LIVES OF HER *FAMILY*. AND EVERY LIVING THING WITHIN A *TWENTY MILE RADIUS*.

CLAIRE JUST HEALED FROM A *HUMAN SKELETON*, BACK INTO A *CHEERLEADER*. THAT'S NOT THE KIND OF THING THAT'S EASY TO *HIDE* FROM THE PEOPLE I WORK FOR. AND FOR THE LAST SIX MONTHS, I'D BEEN *TRYING* TO KEEP CLAIRE'S ABILITIES *UNDER WRAPS*.

YOUR DAUGHTER IS *EXTRAORDINARY*.

I KNOW.

YOU HAVE *ONE HOUR* TO BRING HER IN.

CLAIRE HAD JUST SAVED *THOUSANDS* OF INNOCENT LIVES. I HAD ONE HOUR TO SAVE *HERS*.

THE ONLY PERSON I TRUSTED TO *HELP* ME WAS A WOMAN I HAD *TRAINED*.

HANA GITELMAN HAD THE MOST EXTRAORDINARY *ABILITY* -- TO SEE AND HEAR EVERY BIT OF DATA ON THE INTERNET, SWIRLING AROUND HER LIKE LEAVES IN THE WIND. I CALLED HER *WIRELESS*.

THEY WERE *CLOSING IN*. I HAD TO GET AN *E-MAIL* OUT.

AND *HOPE*.

AND PRAY THAT SHE WAS *OUT* THERE.

LISTENING.

COME ON... *ANSWER* ME! *ANSWER!*

MAYBE HANA HASN'T *FORGIVEN* ME FOR TRICKING HER INTO WORKING FOR THE *BAD GUYS*, AND LEAVING HER FOR *DEAD* IN THE MIDDLE OF THE SERENGETI.

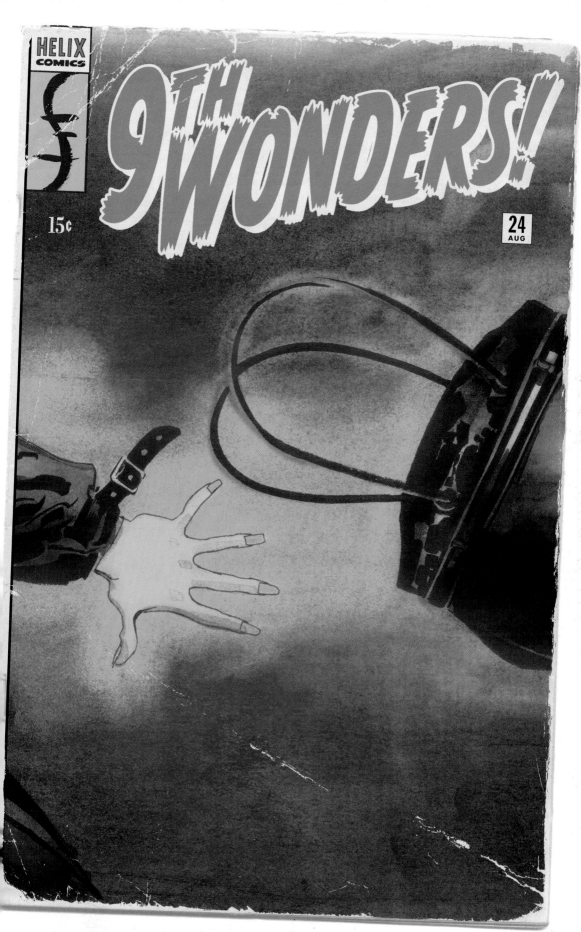

MY NAME IS *HANA GITELMAN*. I CAN SEE, HEAR AND MANIPULATE THE VORTEX OF *WIRELESS DIGITAL INFORMATION* SWIRLING AROUND THE EARTH.

YES, I KNOW. I'M A *WALKING BLACKBERRY*.

WAR BUDDIES
THE LONESTAR FILE

Part 1 *of Six*

DO I *TRUST* HIM?

YESTERDAY, I WANTED *VENGEANCE* ON THE MAN IN THE HORN-RIMMED GLASSES -- *BENNET*.

HE *MANIPULATED* ME. *USED* ME. AND WHEN I NEEDED HIM MOST -- HE THREW ME TO THE *WOLVES*.

TODAY, HE TURNED TO ME FOR *HELP*. SO THE QUESTION IS --

| **MARK WARSHAW** *Story* | **STEVEN LEJEUNE** *Art* | **EDGAR DELGADO** *Colors* **COMICRAFT** *Lettering* |

BENNET SAYS THAT *HE'S* A *VICTIM* TOO. MANIPULATED BY THE COMPANY.

THAT WE'RE BOTH ON THE SIDE OF THE *ANGELS*. THAT IT'S UP TO *US* TO TAKE DOWN THE COMPANY.

TO HELP ME -- BENNET GAVE ME ONE *FILE NUMBER*. THAT'S IT. *ONE*. ACCORDING TO HIM, ONE FILE WOULD HELP ME TAKE DOWN THE *ENTIRE KINGDOM*.

THE *FILE* IS NOT A PROBLEM. IF IT'S BEEN CONVERTED TO A BYTE OR A BIT, I CAN *FIND* IT. NO MATTER *HOW* PAINSTAKINGLY ENCODED.

SEA:V5J1K2/P/L

STORAGE TYPE: PAPER

BUT EVEN *I* HAVE MY LIMITS.

AND I WAS OUT OF *OPTIONS*. SO, REALLY -- WHAT *CHOICE* DID I HAVE?

DON'T BE *MAD* AT ME.

A GIRL'S GOTTA *DO* WHAT A GIRL'S GOTTA *DO.*

WHAT DID YOU *EXPECT?* THAT I'D BREAK INTO THE PENTAGON *GUNS A' BLAZING?*

I NEED TO ACCOMPLISH THIS *MISSION.*

I NEED *ANSWERS* TO MY QUESTIONS.

LOOKS LIKE I'M OFF TO A *GOOD START.*

To Be Continued...

Date: November 15, 1968;
Location: Mekong River
Delta, Vietnam.

We were forty miles
into enemy territory,
on a mission to recover
a downed A4 Skyhawk.

Politicians were in Paris trying
to broker peace. Bombing was
supposed to stop a week before.

So according to
the U.S. Military,
the Skyhawk was
never even there.
We had to make
sure that squared
with reality.

To ensure
plausible
deniability,
we didn't
even know
each others'
identities.
No dog tags,
no rank
insignia,
no personal
effects.

To save the
politicians'
good names, we
gave up ours.

We went by names given to
us by Uncle Sam, but that
didn't change who we were...

Mine's DALLAS.

LAREDO. Demolitions
expert. Was plowing his
Dad's farm by age 13.

SAN ANTONIO. Communications.
Heavyweight Gold Gloves
Champ of Kansas City, MO.

AMARILLO. Gunboat
pilot. Had a girl
named Marcy back home.

AUSTIN. Medic.
Always had his nose
buried in a book.

Time spent under the constant threat of death... it brings men together in a way that tosses formalities aside.

Even so, seven days is a long time to go without hearing your name. Distractions only go so far...

THIS TABLE *EVEN?* EVERYTHING KEEPS SLIDING MY WAY.

HELL, DALLAS. I'M *OUT.*

And tensions ran high.

WHATCHA *GOT* THERE?

Something as simple as a book can make a soldier feel as if home is never too far away.

PERSONAL CONTRABAND? THIS IS ENOUGH TO GET YOU *COURT-MARTIALED.*

ALTHOUGH, BEIN' 40 MILES INTO *ENEMY TERRITORY,* YOU'D JUST AS SOON GET THROWN *OVERBOARD.*

But it could also blow our mission.

GOT SOMETHIN' TO *SAY* FOR YOURSELF, SOLDIER?

Truth is, I was just as guilty of possessing personal contraband as he was.

WE ALL NEED TO HOLD ON TO A PIECE OF *OURSELVES* OUT HERE.

I shared a letter from my family with Austin, hoping he would open up...

...ould have ...een here to ...ee our son. ...e took his ...irst steps ...esterday. ...e's going ...o make us ...roud one day.

...but he had nothing.

YOU GOT *FAMILY*, AUSTIN?

NO, SIR. BEEN ON MY OWN FOR A *WHILE* NOW.

PFFFFT

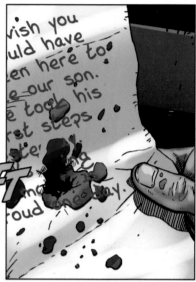

...ish you ...uld have ...een here to ...e our son. ...e took his ...rst steps

...roud one day.

As I showed Austin the letter, our position was compromised to Viet Cong scouts. I took enemy fire to the chest.

Out in the jungle you can lose yourself without even realizing it.

...

And then all that's left is a codename --

Laredo...

SNIPER!

TAT·TAT·TAT·TAT·TAT·TAT·TAT·TAT

Amarillo...

OVER THERE!

TAT·TAT·TAT·TAT·TAT·TAT·TAT

San Antonio...

TAT·TAT·TAT·TAT·TAT·TAT·TAT

During the firefight, the gunboat crew sustained heavy casualties, leaving Austin and myself, ████████ ████████, as the only survivors.

CLEAR!

...AUSTIN...

Sometimes the soldiers you expect the least from, give you the most.

I'd like to go on record, that while there is no evidence to support my statement...

HOLD ON. THE BULLET WENT *CLEAN THROUGH*.

JUST RELAX.

████████████████████
████████████████████

I'VE DONE THIS *BEFORE*.

I never saw a field medic do anything like he did.

It was a miracle.

Day five. Three men down. And I didn't even know their names.

Just aliases. I'm Dallas. Austin, the other survivor, is the medic.

16 kills, still looking for our downed pilots.

AGAIN, WHERE'S THE PLANE?

I DON'T -- ACK!

Patience, along with supplies, was dwindling. We needed answers. Fast.

I wasn't comfortable with Austin. The way he questioned me.

HEAL HIM.

HOW MANY TIMES ARE YOU GONNA DO THIS, DALLAS? IT'S JUST SICK.

The way he could fix people when they should be getting last rites. It wasn't natural.

But it was useful.

JUST DO IT.

Austin applied first aid to the informant as I continued the debriefing.

NOW TELL ME EVERYTHING YOU KNOW...

...OR I BREAK YOUR JAW FOR THE TENTH TIME.

Four hours later, he gave us what we needed.

We reached the plane the next morning. There were no survivors.

We were too late. Our rescue was a failure.

WAR BUDDIES
Part 3 of Six

DJ DOYLE
Story

ADAM ARCHER
Pencils

MARK ROSLAN
Digital Inks

BETH SOTELO
Colors

COMICRAFT
Lettering

NO MORE BULLETS LEFT. HE PUT UP A *FIGHT* AT LEAST.

BRING THEM *BACK.*

YOU KNOW I *CAN'T.* I CAN ONLY HEAL THE *LIVING.*

FREAK.

FREAK? YOU COULDN'T *HANDLE* THE *PAIN* THIS HAS BROUGHT ME.

"THE LAST NIGHT I WAS IN MY HOME, MY MOTHER WAS ON HER *DEATHBED*. LIVER CANCER. HER ORGANS WERE FAILING ONE BY ONE.

"I HELD ON TO HER SO TIGHT. I DIDN'T WANT HER TO *GO*. I WOULD HAVE GIVEN *ANYTHING* TO HELP HER.

"AND SOMEHOW, I *DID*."

GOD HAS ANSWERED MY PRAYERS!

IT WASN'T GOD. IT WAS *ME*.

"THEY DIDN'T HAVE TO *SAY* ANYTHING.

"EVERY TIME THEY *LOOKED* AT ME, I FELT THEIR *FEAR*.

"I COULDN'T *STAND* IT.

"I *LEFT*.

167

I HADN'T HEALED ANYONE ELSE SINCE THEN. TILL *YOU.* AND NOW YOU'VE GOT THAT SAME *LOOK* IN YOUR EYE.

It was unnerving to listen to Austin carry on. I had to focus on something productive.

SIR, WHAT ARE YOU *DOING?*

COME WITH ME.

I PIECED IT TOGETHER FROM MY *NOTES* AND THE *MAP...* WE'RE CLOSE TO THE SKYHAWK'S TARGET: *AU CO.*

But I had no idea how close. The plane had crashed right on the doorstep of its target.

IT'S *PARADISE.*

I elected to carry out Skyhawk's original mission. Austin and I would destroy Au Co ourselves.

YOU CAN'T SCREW WITH *LIVE ORDINANCE!* WE'VE GOT TO GO *BACK.* THERE'S NO ONE *LEFT* HERE TO SAVE.

AU CO ISN'T A *WEAPON!* IT'S NOT A *KILLER!* IT'S A *FARMING VILLAGE!*

WHEN ARE YOU GOING TO FIGURE OUT THAT THIS IS *WAR?*

IT'S NOT WAR *ANYMORE.* PEACE TALKS ARE BEING HELD AS WE SPEAK.

WE JUST HAVE TO KEEP AS MANY OF OUR PEOPLE ALIVE UNTIL WE CAN GET *OUT* OF THIS DAMN COUNTRY.

YOU WANT TO *SAVE* PEOPLE? LOOK DOWN THERE. THAT VILLAGE FEEDS *V.C. ARMIES!* MAYBE *THOUSANDS* OF MEN!

NOW WE CAN GO HOME *TODAY,* HAVING LOST THREE MEN AND HELPED *NO ONE.*

"YOU'LL GET REDEPLOYED INTO ANOTHER *SQUAD,* WHERE MAYBE YOU CAN SAVE A MAN OR TWO IN THE *MUD* DURING BATTLE.

"OR...

YOU TAKE THIS *RIFLE* AND HELP ME RIG THESE *BOMBS.* WE'LL GRIND THEIR WHOLE DAMN WAR EFFORT TO A *HALT.*

AUSTIN, YOU CAN SAVE A FEW *DOZEN* SOLDIERS. OR WE CAN SAVE *THOUSANDS* OF LIVES. IT'S UP TO *YOU.*

I'M IN.

To Be CONTINUED...

What happened at the river and plane would not go unavenged. With C4 explosives from the plane and 7 clips of ammunition between us: the village of Au Co was gonna be toast.

WE HEAD IN ON MY MARK. START WITH THE HUT ON THE FAR LEFT, I'LL START AT THE RIGHT. MEET IN THE MIDDLE.

LOOKS LIKE A LOT OF CIVILIANS.

This was our new mission. With "Austin," a man whose real name I didn't even know. To end the war.

But to him, I was "Dallas." Government code name for government code name. I guess that made it fair.

YEAH? AND WHAT KIND OF CIVILIAN CARRIES A M-16?

"IT DOESN'T ADD UP. THEY'D NEED ALL KINDS OF EQUIPMENT TO FARM THIS MUCH LAND."

The truth was -- the entire valley was created by ███████████████████

██████████████████████ -- it was clear they had unconventional methods.

I could see this affected Austin. His judgement was weakening. He felt connected to this girl.

OH MY GOD, SHE'S --

THE *ENEMY*.

YOU'RE CRAZY.

Austin was ready to abort -- he was losing focus, pulled into emotion.

WHO ARE *YOU* CALLIN' CRAZY? I'M THINKING CLEAR AS DAY. DON'T YOU GET IT?

THIS VILLAGE STAYS IN OPERATION, AND THIS WAR CONTINUES! OUR GUYS DIED TRYING TO END THIS THING! NOW --

YOU *WILL* GO IN THERE AND TAKE OUT THIS VILLAGE. THAT IS A DIRECT COMMAND. DO YOU COPY THAT, SOLDIER?

YES.

YES WHAT?

YES, SIR.

GRAB THE EXPLOSIVES.

We had enough explosives to blow up half the village, get them running -- the fires would take care of the rest.

RIG THE NEXT THREE AND STAND BY. AT 15:30 LIGHT THIS PLACE UP. I'LL BE DIRECTLY ACROSS.

COPY THAT.

The village was heavily armed.

THWACK

We had to be perfect. We had to be brutal.

FOUR...

THREE...

TWO...

ONE...

15:29:57

15:29:58

15:29:59

We had to be willing to risk everything. And that's when it all went wrong.

AU CO!

NO!

Au Co wasn't the village. It was the girl.

We were sent to kill a little girl.

LET HER GO!

GET OFF ME!

CRUNCH

It's like I said. You could really lose yourself out here.

THIS WAR DIES WITH HER.

BRAM

To Be CONTINUED...

A secret mission to find one of
our downed jets turned into taking
out an entire enemy village. We all
thought Au Co was the name of the
village. It wasn't. It was a girl.
I had to kill her.

Au Co, ████████████ with
just a wave of her arms.

WAR BUDDIES
Part 5 of Six INTRODUCTIONS

HARRISON WILCOX
& OLIVER GRIGSBY
Story

JASON BADOWER
Pencils

ANNETTE KWOK
Digital Inks & Colors

COMICRAFT
Lettering

Days earlier, most of the unit was gunned down. Only Austin the medic and I were left. I was shot in the chest.

I should have died.

Austin ████████████████████ ██████ No scars, no blood. Nothing. I should be dead.

He didn't want to go through with the mission. To kill Au Co. Understandable. ████████████████████████ she was special.

But Austin couldn't see the bigger picture.

Au Co had to die. I wouldn't let him save her. Not like he saved me.

YOU'LL THANK ME FOR THIS ONE DAY. WE JUST SAVED A LOT OF LIVES.

With our mission completed, we returned to camp and reported to our superior.

However, there were certain details of the mission that Austin refused to admit to.

I have decided to give full disclosure in this report. Although some might consider me crazy. The things that Austin can do ▮▮▮▮▮▮▮▮▮▮▮▮▮▮▮ essential to the Army.

AM I TO BELIEVE THIS REPORT, SERGEANT?

SIR, I BELIEVE THE SERGEANT MAY BE DELUSIONAL.

WHY WON'T YOU TELL THEM THE *TRUTH?*

THE TRUTH ABOUT *WHAT?*

WHAK

Austin's refusal to admit the truth ended up costing me greatly.

Silenced. Discharged. Ignored. The desire to ▓▓▓▓▓▓▓▓▓▓▓▓ destroyed everything I had built for myself in the military.

My life, my family, for what it was, had become...pointless.

DING DONG

Until Austin showed up at my home. Older and different. With what appeared to be a change of heart.

I OWE YOU AN APOLOGY.

BENNET LED ME TO THIS FILE.

WAR BUDDIES

Part 6 of Six

CALL TO ARMS

HE SAID FINDING IT WOULD PUT US ON THE PATH TO *ANSWERS*.

SEEMS HE WANTED ME TO SEE THE *CONNECTION* BETWEEN THESE TWO MEN.

I JUST DID A SEARCH FOR THIS *LINDERMAN* GUY.

LOOKS LIKE HE IS A *BIG SHOT* OUT OF *VEGAS*.

MARK WARSHAW
Story

STAZ JOHNSON
Pencils

EDGAR AT STUDIO F
Digital Inks & Colors

COMICRAFT *Lettering*

Codename "Dallas": Petrelli.
Codename "Austin": Linderman.

At date of filing, the two men remain close friends.

GUESS WE KNOW WHERE ALL THOSE *ENCODED MESSAGES* OUT OF ODESSA WERE HEADED.

GUESS WE KNOW WHERE I'M HEADED *NEXT*.

CASEY SMITH'S APARTMENT.

I'VE GOT WHAT I *NEED.*

HAD MORE TIME THAN I *EXPECTED* HERE.

SAMANTHA?

MY NEW FRIEND CASEY MUST BE A *DEEP SLEEPER.*

I NEED TO REPORT A POSSIBLE *HIGH LEVEL SECURITY BREACH,* SIR!

FROM: CaseyZ

My bad, Sir. Just found my ID card in the washing machine. Sorry for the false alarm. Be in soon to explain myself.

STAND DOWN. FALSE ALARM.

MORE EXCITEMENT THAN WE'VE HAD IN *WEEKS*.

TIME TO GET THE HELL *OUT* OF HERE.

ARCHIVES

RONALD REAGAN INTERNATIONAL AIRPORT. WASHINGTON, DC.

Auto Check in

Auto Check

Stateside
Auto Check in

GETTING LINDERMAN'S CREDIT CARD NUMBER WASN'T THAT TOUGH. BREAKING THRU HIS *FIREWALL* IS A DIFFERENT STORY.

Flight 36
Destination:
Las Vegas, NV
Account Billing Info:
Linderman Group
Group Card Number:
567 12

HE HAS BETTER *ENCRYPTION PROTOCOLS* THAN THE *US GOVERNMENT.*

THAT *SAYS* SOMETHING. IT SAYS YOU HAVE SOMETHING TO *HIDE.* IT SAYS YOU ARE A REAL *SHADY* BASTARD.

I'LL NEED TO BE AT *CLOSER RANGE* IF I AM GOING TO BE ABLE TO DIG *DEEPER.*

I'LL COME BACK FOR THE *BIKE.* I DON'T WANT TO WASTE ANY *TIME.*

Stateside

I'M INTO HIS SERVER *NOW.* LOOKING FOR ANYTHING WITH THE NAME *"PETRELLI".*

NATHAN PETRELLI

New York Election Results Assurance

ELECTION RIGGING. THIS GUY REALLY IS A *PEACH.*

IF THIS LINDERMAN GUY WANTS PETRELLI TO WIN SO BAD, IT *CAN'T* BE A GOOD THING.

TO UNRIG AN ELECTION IS A *TALL ORDER.*

I'M GOING TO NEED A LITTLE HELP FROM MY *FRIENDS.*

WANT TO HELP HANA RUIN LINDERMAN'S PLANS? FOLLOW THE DIRECTIONS IN THE TEXT MESSAGE OR E-MAIL TITLED *"CALL TO ARMS"* FOR NEXT STEPS.

IF YOU ARE NOT A REGISTERED HEROES 360 USER, GO HERE: www.samantha48616e61.com *TO JOIN THE CAUSE NOW!*

NEW YORK CITY. THE FUTURE.

IT WAS THE EVE OF THE ANNIVERSARY.

FIVE YEARS AFTER THE EXPLOSION DECIMATED HALF THE CITY.

I DON'T WANT TO *HURT* YOU. GET BACK IN YOUR CRUISER AND GET YOUR MEN OFF THE STREETS.

OKAY. YEAH. WHATEVER YOU SAY...

BUT IT FELT JUST LIKE ANY OTHER NIGHT.

I WAS TRYING TO KEEP MY *OWN* SAFE.

SPARROW, HOW MANY TIMES DO I NEED TO *TELL* YOU? CURFEW MEANS CURFEW.

SAYS *WHO*? THE GOVERN-MENT?

SAYS *ME*. NOW GET HOME. *QUICK*.

I TRIED NOT TO THINK ABOUT THE SAD TRUTH.

THAT WE WERE LOSING.

MAYBE WE'D ALREADY LOST.

AFTER THE BOMB WENT OFF, PEOPLE LIKE *ME* -- SPECIAL PEOPLE -- WE BECAME *HATED.* HUNTED. SECOND CLASS CITIZENS.

I WANTED TO CHANGE IT. I *NEEDED* TO.

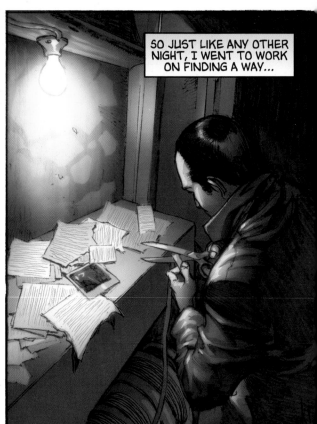

SO JUST LIKE ANY OTHER NIGHT, I WENT TO WORK ON FINDING A WAY...

...I WENT TO WORK ON THE *STRINGS.*

String Theory

JOE POKASKI
Story

STAZ JOHNSON
Pencils

EDGAR AT STUDIO F *Digital Inks & Colors*

COMICRAFT *Lettering*

AFTER FIVE YEARS OF MANIPULATING TIME, I BEGAN TO *UNDERSTAND* IT.

TIME WAS NOT A LINE OR A FABRIC, BUT THE PRODUCT OF LIVES, INTERWEAVED.

SYLAR'S LIFELINE WAS CRUCIAL, OF COURSE. HE WAS THE *BOMB.*

I STABBED HIM BEFORE HE EXPLODED, BUT HE *REGENERATED.*

HE WAS ABLE TO DO THIS BECAUSE HE KILLED *CLAIRE BENNET,* THE CHEERLEADER.

SO TO SAVE THE WORLD, I NEEDED TO FIND SOMEONE FROM *THAT* TIME TO SAVE THE CHEERLEADER.

SOMEONE I KNEW WOULD *NOT FAIL.*

PETER PETRELLI.

193

THIS IS THE *SPOT.*

BUT NOT THE *TIME.*

SO I TRAVELED FIVE YEARS INTO THE *PAST.*

TO THIS FATEFUL MOMENT.

PETER PETRELLI.

HOW IS THIS HAPPENING?

I'M SORRY IF I *SCARED* YOU...

WHERE I DELIVERED A MESSAGE TO PETER.

WALLS Part 1

JOE POKASKI
Story

TOM GRUMMETT
Art

CHRIS SOTOMAYOR Colors
COMICRAFT Lettering

TWO GUARDS MANNED THE BACK ENTRANCE. WE *FROZE TIME,* NO PROBLEM.

THEY HAD WHAT WE *NEEDED* TO GET INSIDE.

FROM THERE, WE *SPLIT UP.*

HIRO MADE HIS WAY TO THE MAIN *CONTROL CENTER.*

HE WOULD DISABLE THE *LOCKS* ON ALL THE THE DOORS.

BUT ONCE HE *DID,* WE COULDN'T FREEZE *TIME* ANYMORE.

WE NEEDED TO MOVE IN *REAL TIME.*

OTHERWISE WE'D HAVE TO DRAG OUT A LOT OF STIFF *TIME-FROZEN* BODIES.

JUST SHY OF *TWO HUNDRED.*

MY NAME IS *NIKI SANDERS.*

AND I'VE LIVED A *LOT* OF LIVES.

BEEN A LOT OF THINGS.

AN ABUSED DAUGHTER. AN ALCOHOLIC.

A STRIPPER. AN UNWILLING MURDERER.

A WIFE. A MOTHER. A SURVIVOR. A MOURNER.

AND NOW, FOR THE SECOND TIME, AN *INMATE.*

BUT SAVE AN ISOLATED INCIDENT OR TWO...

...I WAS NEVER REALLY A *FIGHTER.*

THIS WAS *NEW.*

THANKS.

ALL I KNEW WAS HIS NAME. *PETER.*

LIGHTNING. THAT OUGHT TO COME IN HANDY.

HE AND HIS *LITTLE FRIEND* WERE BREAKING US OUT.

TRYING TO, ANYWAY.

WHY CAN'T WE *FREEZE* TIME?

ONE OF THEM MUST BE ABLE TO *BLOCK* IT SOMEHOW.

WHICH *ONE?*

I HOPE YOU *ENJOYED* THAT LAST BREATH. BECAUSE IT'S, WELL...YOUR *LAST BREATH.*

YOU *TOUCH* HER AND IT WILL BE *YOURS* TOO.

YOU CAN'T BURN WHAT YOU CAN'T *CATCH,* SCAR-BOY.

WELL, THANKS TO OUR *QUALITY TIME* TOGETHER, I'M AS *FAST* AS *YOU* ARE.

TALK ABOUT SPEED-DATING...

MAYBE I SHOULD HAVE *STAYED* IN LOCK-UP.

AT LEAST IN THERE, NO ONE WAS TRYING TO *KILL* ME.

AT LEAST I KNEW WHO I WAS -- *PRISONER NIKI.*

I'VE BEEN A LOT OF THINGS.

LIVED A LOT OF LIVES.

PICKED UP A FEW TRICKS FROM *EACH* OF THEM, I SUPPOSE.

BUT *NEVER*, IN A MILLION YEARS, WOULD I HAVE GUESSED, THAT OF *ALL THINGS...*

...IT WOULD BE THE *POLE-DANCING* THAT WOULD SAVE MY HIDE.

WALLS Part 2

JOE POKASKI
Story

MICHAEL GAYDOS
Art

EDGAR AT STUDIO F *Colors*
COMICRAFT *Lettering*

AND JUST LIKE *THAT,* WE LEFT.

WE WERE *FREE.*

SORT OF.

WHEN CAN I TALK TO MY *WIFE?*

YOU ARE ALL STILL IN *DANGER.*

WE'RE GOING TO ARRANGE TRANSPORTATION TO A SPECIAL FACILITY IN TEXAS...

WHAT'S IN *TEXAS?*

MOST OF MY FELLOW INMATES HAD FAMILIES TO REUNITE WITH. *LIVES* TO RESUME.

I HAD *NO IDEA* WHAT TO DO NEXT.

YOU WERE *GREAT* BACK THERE, BY THE WAY.

THANKS.

I'VE LIVED A LOT OF LIVES.

LET ME KNOW IF YOU NEED ANY *HELP* WITH ANYTHING... LIKE TRACKING DOWN YOUR *FAMILY.*

THAT'S NOT NECESSARY. I DON'T REALLY *HAVE* A FAMILY ANYMORE.

OH.

BUT THEY ALL *ENDED* THE DAY THE *BOMB* WENT OFF.

WHO WOULD I BECOME *NOW?*

WHEN I WAS A LITTLE GIRL, I IMAGINED HEAVEN WAS FILLED WITH CLOUDS AND ANGELS WITH BEAUTIFUL FEATHERED WINGS.

THE HEAVENS ARE FILLED WITH MECHANICAL ANGELS -- *SATELLITES.* THOUSANDS AND THOUSANDS OF SATELLITES.

AND LIKE ANGELS -- THEY WATCH OVER US. THEY SEE EVERYTHING WE DO. EVERY CALL WE MAKE. EVERY E-MAIL WE WRITE. THEY KNOW HOW WE LIVE.

SEARCHING... TARGET: HANA GITELMAN...

AND THEY KNOW HOW WE *DIE.*

NOTHING IS WHAT I EVER EXPECTED.

THREE DAYS AGO. SOMEWHERE BETWEEN TEXAS AND NEW YORK.

HANA.

I WASN'T SURE IF YOU GOT MY MESSAGE. WE NEED TO TALK.

I DIDN'T WANT TO.

I'M GETTING A LITTLE SICK OF FOLLOWING YOUR ORDERS. I MEAN, HOW CAN WE TRUST YOUR ENDGAME?

BENNET HAS US ALL WRAPPED AROUND HIS LITTLE FINGER. JUMPING THROUGH HOOPS. DOING YOUR DIRTY WORK.

I'M TRYING TO HELP YOU GET YOUR LIFE BACK TO NORMAL.

MY LIFE HAS NEVER BEEN NORMAL. THANKS TO YOU, IT NEVER WILL BE.

ACCORDING TO NEWS REPORTS THAT DAY, MANY CELL PHONES AND E-MAIL PROVIDERS SAID THE TEMPORARY *GLITCH* IN SERVICE WAS DUE TO *MAGNETIC ACTIVITY.*

I KNEW IT WAS BECAUSE OF *ME.*

...AND I'M *NOT* ABOUT TO GO DOWN WITHOUT A *FIGHT.*

THE *DEATH* OF HANA GITELMAN

ARON ELI COLEITE
Story

JASON BADOWER
Art & Color

COMICRAFT
Lettering

Part 2

EVEN IN MY WILDEST DREAMS, I *NEVER* EXPECTED TO BE DOING *THIS...*

THIS IS HOW THE *ANGELS* SEE THE EARTH -- OBSERVING -- WATCHING -- *EVERYTHING.*

AND FOR A MOMENT I *FORGET* ABOUT THE MISSION. AND I FORGET ABOUT THE *MANIPULATIONS.* AND THE PAIN. AND THE *DEATH.*

I *HAD* TO DO IT. IT WAS THE ONLY *CHOICE.* IT WAS THE ONLY WAY THAT PEOPLE LIKE ME COULD BE *SAFE.*

AND I DIDN'T *WANT* TO BE A MARTYR. AND I WASN'T DOING IT FOR *REVENGE,* OR BECAUSE I HAD A *DEATH WISH.* I DID IT BECAUSE IT WAS THE *RIGHT THING* TO DO.

SO, I SUPPOSE IN A LOT OF WAYS -- IT'S *EXACTLY* HOW I EXPECTED TO DIE.

SAMANTHA48616:
...THE JOURNEY IS JUST BEGINNING.

JEPH: A comic book version of HEROES seems like a no-brainer, but how did it come about?

ARON & JOE: If Tim Kring was the general who ordered a strike on the American zeitgeist with this crazy show called "Heroes"—I guess you could consider us to be some of the first boots on the ground. Before the Pilot was even picked up, we talked extensively with Tim about the online component of the show. How to extend the storytelling from one hour on a Monday into an immersive fan experience.

The online comic was one of the first ideas that came to mind. We had so many stories to tell and there was only so much room in the TV show—so we decided that we could tell these alternate stories in the comics. The stories could be deeper, broader and reveal more secrets about our characters. It was also a way to tell stories that would be otherwise unproduceable on our show.

But this is different from traditional comics, right? It's online and only 5 or 6 pages a shot.

The goal was to put out 22 pages a month, like most comics, but to come out weekly like a television show. So the math dictated 5 or 6 pages per installment and we lucked into the perfect length for a Heroes Webcomic.

Like the scenes or stories in the pilot or in subsequent episodes—the webcomic would be what we called "Haiku," short but purposeful. Every panel meaning something.

It actually forced us to be better, more concise storytellers—we weren't allowed to ramble or wander. We had to tell unique, exciting and fulfilling stories in 5 pages.

You've filled in some of the gaps in the stories from the show. Do you feel like people who watch the show have to read these to know what's going on?

Not at all. In fact, our first rule going in was that you didn't have to read the comic to enjoy the show, but it created an enhanced experience if you did.

On the other side, we wanted people who did watch the show and read the comic to feel rewarded—that they were taking part of something larger and give them real emotional and important stories—not just fluff or filler.

Michael Turner, Phil Jimenez, Aspen, Nanci Quesada, Alex Ross, and Jim Lee—and those are just for starters. How did the comic book community get involved with what could otherwise be seen as just another licensed property?

For starters, we had a big gun—this guy named Jeph Loeb. It's not a stretch to call him a living legend. And on top of that, a ridiculously large amount of people in the industry who love him—and would jump in front of a train for him. We're not sure if it was that, or his ability to sell a good idea, but soon we had an amazing bullpen of writers and artists working for us.

The short format had a little to do with it too. Many comic book artists pour their hearts and soul onto each page. At 22 pages per comic that is a lot of soul pouring. It's easier to get a top-notch artist for 5 or 6 pages. It's like keeping a friend out at a bar by saying "one more drink." Who doesn't want one more?

Are there new writers we can look forward to next season?

We've already got a bunch of great writers from the show. We've also been joined by veterans like Steven Seagle, Joe Kelly and Duncan Rouleau. But, we've also been fortunate to get some young comic book scribes to join our crew like Mark Sable and Christine Boylen.

On top of that, we've got an amazing staff of up and coming brilliant minds that help us with the impossible task of writing one of these a week. Writers like Harry Wilcox, Oliver Grigsby, Chris Zatta, Jim Martin, Pierluigi Cothran, Timm Keppler and Andrew Chambliss. Watch out for these names—you will see them in the future.

And rumor has it that a certain writer whose name rhymes with SCHMEPH SCHMOEB will introduce a new character called "Rachel Red, Robogirl."

You had to start even before anyone had seen the show. What was that like?

In a lot of ways, it was liberating. As with the show, all we could do is tell the most exciting stories that you would want to experience yourself. Just go for it, because there was no audience reaction to be reactionary towards.

But of course, in the back of your head, for the show and the webcomic, there's the whole "what if you threw a Television Show and nobody arrives" concern eating at the back of your head.

Are there some stories you CAN'T or WON'T tell as comics?

We don't want to touch anything that should be seen on the television. For example, we were tempted to tell the webcomic of how H.R.G. got assigned to be Claire's father—but we knew that would be better served on the show—as everyone finally saw in "Company Man."

There's a new online story up every week! How do you do that when some monthly comics ¿koff-*Ultimates*-koff¿ sometimes can't make shipping!

Most of that lies with a guy named Mark Warshaw. And Chuck Kim. They keep the trains running on time. Sometimes we run right up to the wire and deliver the pages moments before they need to go live, but even so—we have yet to miss a deadline.

Fortunately we're able to line up the stories with the episodes so we can try to keep ahead of the curve and have scripts generated quickly and early.

If you could have a crossover with any of the DC characters, what would your dream team-up be?

I think everyone would want to see the Supergirl/Claire team up. A Peter/Superman throwdown might be fun as well. And of course Green Lantern/Ando would be a classic matchup.

So...are you comic book writers or graphic novelists? Remember, this is how you'll be defined for the rest of your lives...

Is there a third choice?

You're both pretty big comic geeks. What's it like now, creating your own universe? What do you read? Do you buy comics on a weekly basis?

Each Wednesday (ideally) we actually make our trek to the local store. A big shout-out to our friends at Meltdown who take good care of us every week. We read a lot of everything. Bendis. Millar. Johns. And of course everything that Loeb puts out. It's one of the rare pleasures in life to go to a comic book store with Jeph Loeb and see the fans pointing and whispering.

Are there stories that you can tell only in this graphic novel form?

There are certainly ones that are easier—because there are no production restraints. For example, when Hana Gitelman went to China to stow away on the Space Shuttle so she could spacewalk to a satellite and ride it down into the burning atmosphere. That would have been difficult to produce.

Fire. Space. Polar Ice Caps. Jungles of Africa. Battles with Indian gods and confrontations with Australian rock formations. There is no limit in this format. It's very rewarding.

ALAN MOORE

TAKES ON A WHOLE NEW UNIVERSE!

0

In 1992 Jim Lee and Brandon Choi ushered in a new era of in comics with the release of WildC.A.Ts #1. It introduced readers to the WildStorm Universe and was a runaway sensation. Several years later Alan Moore and Travis Charest tried their hands at the WildStorm flagship title and the results were astounding; Moore's unique stories coupled with Charest's masterful visuals set a new bar for the title.

Now, for the first time, Moore's complete story is collected in one handsome volume, telling the entire WildC.A.T.s saga that he envisioned from start to finish. It's a tale of honor, adventure and betrayal, as only the writer of WATCHMEN, V FOR VENDETTA and THE LEAGUE OF EXTRAORDINARY GENTLEMEN could tell it!

THE AMERICAN WAY

RIDLEY•JEANTY

RED MENACE

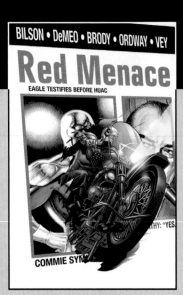

**BILSON•DeMEO•
BRODY•ORDWAY•VEY**

STORMWATCH: PHD
BOOK 1

GAGE•MAHNKE

MIDNIGHTER

**ENNIS•SPROUSE•
FABRY•STORY**

WELCOME TO
TRANQUILITY

SIMONE•GOOGE

SUPERNATURAL:
ORIGINS

**JOHNSON•SMITH
(APRIL 2008)**